ANCHORS &
VACANCIES
KAT SAVAGE

ANCHORS & VACANCIES

ISBN-13: 978-1533424389
ISBN-10: 1533424381

HELLO!

This is a collection of work originally titled
"Left Atrium Anchors & Right Ventricle Vacancies"
that I wrote from the end of 2014 to early 2015.
I was having a really rough go with love
and I wanted to express how I was feeling.

So, this is for all of you.
I know you hurt.
I've hurt, too.

1

There's a certain kind of ache
in the vacant chambers of my heart,
like a slow bleed foreshadowing the
death of something that never really lived.

My body pleads with itself
to remember what it was like
before all it did was miss you.

2

Sometimes I hold onto things
I have no business holding onto.
They become a part of me
the way I hoped they would.
But when it's time for them to go,
they simply don't.

Memories of you are thick
on my skin and I can't seem to
wash them away.
You should've peeled them off
and packed them up
with everything else
when you left.

3

You weren't the settling down type
and I knew that going in.
I actually thought I was going to be
the thing that changed you.
Or maybe I was hopelessly hoping.
We all have those kinds of pipe dreams.
One good gust of wind
and you were lost to me.
I never understood how losing something
that wasn't mine to begin with
left me more empty than when I found it.

4

I've lost count of how many times
I've come crawling back to you,
hoping for something within you
to be moved.
I didn't need it all,
I just wanted a little piece of you
to call my own.
Alas—
you remain whole,
and I am the one in pieces.

5

My lungs are brown paper bags
and I can hear them fold in on themselves
every time I lose my breath
to the memory of the first time
you kissed me.
And I know sooner or later
they're going to catch fire
and leave soot smeared across
my birdcage ribs.

6

I know somewhere
you have my heart in an exhibit,
with pins holding it open on display
in one of those cases that usually
keeps beautiful dead butterflies.
I know you like to watch as it
struggles through the agony—
still trying to beat for you
in all its reckless glory.

7

Please don't tell me you miss me.
I simply don't have the strength
to lie to you this morning—
to tell you I don't miss you in return.

8

I remember when you held me
like maybe I was the only thing that
mattered—
and maybe I was in that moment.
Now,
you hold her with that same look
in your eyes.
And it was then that I realized
your bones weren't built
for devotion.

9

I toss and turn
in the still of the night.
The empty spot in the bed next to me
mimics the empty spot inside me.
Your absence is everywhere.
I flip the pillow over to feel the cold side—
it mimics your heart.

10

The only thing I've ever
been sure of
in my entire miserable existence,
is that I was meant to love you.
I don't know for how long
or even in what way.
I just know it's written in the lines
on the palms of my hands.
So take hold of them.
Take hold of me.

11

The clock ticks
and the sun sets
and the moon rises.
Cars drive by.
The weatherman says
it's supposed to be sunny tomorrow.
The bottle is growing emptier.
All the while I sit here
missing the parts of me
I lost to you.

12

I didn't really think I could save you.
I thought at best we'd have some
laughs
and kisses
and moments
of *maybe.*
And you'll think for a second that
maybe you could feel something
for me
but that's when you'll leave.
And I'll watch the next woman
miraculously save you.
I'd like to think in some way
I had something to do with that.

13

I was just floating
with no purpose,
with nothing to hold me down.
I was in a perpetual state of waiting.
Though, I don't really know
what for.
And then something kind of strange
happened.
I locked eyes with you.
All the empty space inside me
filled up with all the things
I wanted to give you.
I was home.
And I was hoping you were, too.

14

Let's pretend for a moment that
we've known each other longer
than just a few nights.
Let's pretend you already know
my favorite drink at the bar
and what I like on my pizza.
And I'll pretend I know
what side of the bed you prefer
and how you take your coffee in the
morning.
Let's pretend we've already built
all of that up together.
So as we walk down the sidewalk,
hands intertwined,
we can focus on breaking down
the walls that were built up
through all the years
before tonight.

15

All my life,
even being with someone
has been lonely.
I've always been waiting
for the one who knows exactly
how to love me.
My lovely lonely little heart
beats hope,
palpitating toward an unknown horizon.
What good is my heart if not for
the adventure?
The potential of discovering
what it has always been seeking?

16

He wasn't anything special.
Average height,
average weight.
He made me laugh sometimes.
He liked to watch television
while I read a book
with my feet in his lap
and he always had his hands
on them.
It was comfortable.
He had a pretty smile
and pretty brown eyes
even though one was a little lazy.
Sometimes he was nice
but sometimes he was downright
vain.
He wasn't really anything special—
I just really wanted him to be.

17

I crave you
the way the insignificant
flame of a candle
craves oxygen
at the onset of darkness.
I crave you
the only way I have
ever known how—
as if my life depends
on your very existence,
and my death will eventually
be at your hand.

18

I'm not good at this.
This thing that isn't exactly love
and isn't exactly friendship either.
It's messy here in the middle
carrying buckets full of
wasted emotion
you don't want
and I can't reuse.
I don't know how to navigate here.
My compass is broken
and my map is torn.
I don't know how to get from here
to a place where it doesn't hurt
when you tell me
not tonight.

19

Sometimes I feel unsteady,
like I can't find solid footing,
like at any moment I might topple over
into the depths of your shadow
and finally lose all of myself to you.
I've managed to hold onto
just a little bit of me all this time,
the little bit of me I refused to give to you.
I'm slipping now
and it scares the hell out of me.
Please,
hold onto me,
so I don't have to.

20

I begged for your mercy
as you slowly and carefully
awoke within me
all the feelings that had long since
been dead.
To my pleas, you told me
you'd hold me tight
and give me a reason
to believe again.
And you did.
And I did.
In your absence I'm trying to find
my way back to numb,
but feeling everything inside me
die all over again seems to hurt
a little more given it was
born to lies and lived in the shadow
of half-hearted truths.

21

I was lucky enough to have you in my life
for as long as I did.
At least,
I desperately wanted to believe that.
That's the thing about falling in love
with someone who moved like the wind.
I was sad to watch you go,
but would have loved you less
if you had stayed—
if you had clipped your wings
and become something other than
what I fell for.

22

Don't worry about it.
This happens to me all the time.
I am walking toward a horizon,
sun rising,
and each step I take
I think I'm getting closer
to what I've always wanted.
And yet, as I look ahead
I realize I'm only ever further away.
I always fell in love with the
unobtainable
because the hurt was familiar
and in so many ways,
it was safe.

23

I should've known the words
that were coming
long before they left your mouth.
I had become so used to it,
to
"I don't know"
and
"I'm not out but I don't know if I'm in"
but you had one foot out
before you ever took a step toward me.
And if by now I haven't swayed you,
I don't think you're staying.
So go.
Find someone who makes you
want to stay.

24

You asked me if I ever wrote about you
and it killed me that I couldn't say no.
There are pieces of you in all of it.
I had written the beginning and the middle
but mostly the end.
I didn't want to.
I had to.
It was all I could do to feel again.
You asked me if I ever wrote about you
and I didn't want to say yes.
So I said nothing at all.

25

Suddenly I was so sorry
I had let unworthy men
touch this body.
My body.
Suddenly I was so worried
I had let too many come before you
and pull from me anything of worth,
leaving me hollow.
And now,
when it matters most,
I am so afraid
I will have nothing left to give you.
It's so clear you're the only one
who has ever been deserving.

26

The best thing I ever did
was stop begging you to stay
when all you wanted to do was go.
It was dreadfully wonderful,
realizing in the midst of wanting you
that your leaving was what I needed
in order to ignite peace within me.
And these days,
it's easier to discern
between
what I want
and
what I need.

27

It's all right if you don't want to be here
in my life.
I'm not making an effort to keep you in it
when it's quite clear to me
you're just passing through.
And,
if you could stop looping back around
to take a little more of me
each time,
I think I could heal.
I can't let you use me as a pit stop anymore.
I can't let you
come and go
as you please
again.
I know it's not your intention
but I can't.
And I'm not sure which of us
it's going to hurt more.

28

I didn't realize until
halfway through the conversation
that you were speaking in past tense.
"You were lovely"
and
"You were so interesting"
as if
I was no longer those things.
And I wasn't to you.
Not anymore.
I don't know why this shocked me.
I was only ever meant to be the past.
I was going to miss
the idea
of you.
I was already
just a memory
to you.

29

I only ever wanted to be the thing
that calmed your soul
and lit it on fire
at the exact same time.
I only ever sought to
give you all of me.
Your silence has always been
the loudest noise.
I'll be over this one day.
But tonight,
I'll blanket myself
in all my
wants & wishes,
all my sad little lonely tears.
I'll remember I was yours once.
I'll remember.

30

I'm waiting.
Always just waiting
for someone to break
the silent chaos of my mind,
to still all the words flying around.
I'm waiting for someone
to come along
and suddenly all these
lonely nights will make sense.
The silence at night
won't be the torture of lonely
but the peace that comes
at long last with the right one.

31

I don't miss you like I used to.
My mind isn't constantly filled with
thoughts of you and I don't keep
wishing you were mine anymore.
There are no tears cried for you.
And I can't recall the last time
I wondered what you were doing.
No, I don't miss you like I used to.
I miss you
in a completely different way.
With dry eyes and a silent mind.
I don't know which way hurts more.

32

Being with you was never a simple task.
It was never easy,
never relaxed.
A gauntlet of sorts,
you were always trying and testing,
bringing me to my knees.
I was always begging for mercy.
I gave,
I bled.
I fought for your love
but all you ever did was
kick me down
and change the rules
whenever you felt me
getting too close.

33

I wish I knew
where this was going
or how I'll know when I get there
that it's where I'm meant to be.
I'd like to think I will
but everything gets so blurry,
especially around you.
I don't know if that's mostly my fault
or yours.
Maybe,
just maybe,
you like making me fuzzy around the
edges.
Maybe it helps you
focus
on the center.

34

You liked me for a little bit.
Or,
at least I like to think you did.
Maybe that was my mistake all along.
You were curious and I was intriguing
and after you finished solving
the mysteries of me,
suddenly I lacked luster.
Maybe I was only ever going to be
the girl
who was fun to chase
but never worth holding onto.

35

A love like ours
would have singed the sky
and all the stars would've fallen
to their deaths.
I'm convinced that's why
it couldn't last any longer.
Our story was written
long before we started flipping the pages.
We were brief,
but no less beautiful.
And we'd have probably ruined it
if given the chance.
So I'll take the memories
just the way they are.

36

I don't understand
why mountains and rivers
were born between us
and why my hand isn't
closer to yours on cold nights.
I can't figure out why we were split,
made to live in separate places.
It's a bittersweet thing,
knowing someone exists
who is perfect for me
and yet, I will never
be close enough
to know the story
that could've been,
the story
that should've been.

37

When I have time to waste
I doodle your name
in the margins of my notebook
with little hearts and lightning bolts.
I can't help myself.
I know it's silly and
you'll never see it
but part of me thinks
every time I scribble it down,
I'm making a wish,
and maybe if I do it enough
you'll come back to me.

38

I spent the first 73 days
after your last phone call to me
praying you'd make just one more.
I spent the next 56 days after that
accepting it wasn't coming
and realizing I shouldn't waste
any more of my time or prayers on you.
A few days after that,
never mind how many,
I realized nothing lasts forever.
Not you,
but not the ache either.

39

You were never good at staying.
I don't know what made you
leave each time,
but it hurt just the same.
I was always trying to figure out
why you kept coming back.
Your absence shrieks within me
and I can't hear the whispers
of your broken promises anymore.

40

I was waiting for you to say words
you were never going to say,
and I was waiting for you
to touch me in a way
you were never going to,
and I was waiting for a kiss
to soothe the ache in my skin
but it would never know your mouth.
All the best parts of me
want for something
that's never been mine,
something I've never experienced.
I never knew such a pain could exist
for the unknown.

41

Forgive me
if it takes some time
to find the me
who was here before you.
Loving you has been the
beginning and the end
of everything I thought
I knew about myself.
So losing you
meant losing me, too.

42

I am searching for someone,
something,
anything
to gently rip me from the claws
you've so deeply embedded into me.
You have a quiet violence about you,
never giving thought to how much
destruction you cause
to the most tender parts of me.
I haven't the strength
to keep rebuilding
when you make broken
look so damn good.

43

Tell me a lie,
just once.
Tell me you could see us together.
Too many more
I don't knows
and it might be enough
to make me realize
a year into this thing
that it's the only answer you're ever
going to give me.
Once I realize that,
I'll have the strength to leave,
to finally walk away.
So, please,
lie to me.
Just once.
Because I'm not ready
to let go of these delusions
your false gestures
have built up within me.

44

Even on nights like tonight,
when drinks are flowing
and friendly laughs fill the air,
you're still right at the edge
of my thoughts,
begging for attention.

And after enough liquor,
I can't help but
give in
and swim through an ocean
of memories
to find you waiting
on my cognitive shore.

45

It's okay, I will be fine.
I've survived this too many times.
Though I have to wonder
how many times I can blow my own leg off
before it's no longer a leg
and can never be a leg again.
These not-quite, very-nearly lovers
half-hold me for a moment.
They cannot lose me,
do not want all of me,
and I don't know how to break myself
down
into something fractional for them.
These half-lovers—
the almost, just-shy-of-lovers—
they never stay long.
They stay too long.

ABOUT THE AUTHOR

Kat Savage is a single mom of two, works full time, and manages to jot a few words down here and there in her spare time. She has a degree in graphic design and takes advantage of it to design all of her own books plus freelances.

Kat Savage is very active on social media and wants you to semi-stalk her.

Follow her on Instagram:
@kat.savage

Like her on Facebook:
Facebook.com/katsavagepoetry

Tweet her on Twitter:
@thekatsavage

Connect with her:
www.thekatsavage.com

Made in the USA
Lexington, KY
09 December 2016